Camping Hiking E   ;t
This bo

Name	
Email	
Telephone	
Address	

This book is copyright materials by
@Vanessa Robins

Checklist for Camping

Check	Listing
	Tent (With Stakes and guylines)
	Tent footprint
	Repair kit for pads, mattress, tent, tarp
	Sun Shade Tarp Screen House
	Sleeping bag for each camper
	Sleeping Pad for each camper
	Pillows
	Blanket with some extra
	Air Mattress
	Pump for air mattress
	Knifes set and or multi tools set
	Day pack or day bag
	Roller Jogger
	Trekking pole
	Child carrier
	Chair or folding chair
	Folding table and table cloth
	Cots
	Hammer and some other tools
	Headlamp with batteries
	Lantern or lamp and fuel or batteries
	Water filter
	Bike/bike trailer
	Canoe or kayak gear
	Fishing gear
	Flash lights
	Small Shovel

Checklist for Clothing

Check	Listing
	Daytime clothing
	Night time clothing
	Swimsuits
	Rain Coat
	Long Sleeve shirt
	Sun Shielding Hat
	Buffs
	Shoes: hiking/walking shoes, easy-on shoes, water shoes.
	Boot
	Sock
	Long Underwear
	Insulating Vest or Jackets
	Rainwear: Jacket and Pants
	Clothesline with Clip
	Sandal or booties for in-camp wear
	Gloves
	Hats
	Quick drying shorts and pants
	Water Sandals

Checklist for Kitchen 1

Check	Listing
	Stove
	Fuel for stove
	Windscreen
	Fuel bottles with fuel panel
	Matches or lighter
	Firewood source near campsite
	Charcoal
	Frying pan
	Cook Pot and pot grabber
	Portable coffee maker
	Grill rack
	Hot and cold vacuum bottle
	Hand crank blender
	Corkscrew/bottle opener/can opener
	Roasting sticks for marshmallows, hot dogs
	Food storage container and bags
	Trash bag
	Cooler
	Resealable storage bag
	Water bottles
	Plates, bowls, mixing bowl, Forks, spoons, knives set for cooking
	Cups, Mugs
	Paring knives, spatula, cooking spoon
	Utensil
	Cutting board
	Sponge, dishcloth, dish towel
	Soap for dish wash

Checklist for Kitchen 2

Check	Listing
	Paper towel
	Foil
	Kitchen organizer
	Funnel
	Egg Holder
	Collapsible water container
	Portable or standing camp sink
	Drying rack
	Resealable storage bag
	Others on your own design

Checklist for Foods

Check	Listing
	Coffee/Tea/milk/chocolate/cacao
	Cereal/cornflake/granola/oatmeal
	Eggs
	Breakfast bar
	Batter mix
	Syrup/Jelly/Jam
	Butter/Margarine/Cheese
	Bread
	Soup mix/bouillon cubes
	Cooking oil/Spray
	Salt/pepper
	Drink mixes
	Bottles/Cans/beverage
	Fruits
	Vegetables
	Energy food (Bat/Cereal)
	Crackers/Chips
	Chocolate/Sweet
	Marshmallows
	Spice Kits
	Herbs
	Meat at your choice
	Pancake mix
	Serving Tray
	BBQ tools
	Plastic wave

Personal Checklist

Check	Listing
	Toilet paper
	Sunscreen/lotion
	First Aids-kits
	Lips balm
	Prescription medication
	Insect Repellent
	Hand Sanitizer
	Alcohol or antiseptic wipe
	Toothbrush/toothpaste
	Toiletries
	Soap
	Menstrual and urinary products
	Brush
	Comb
	Hair clip
	Cosmetic
	Eyeshades
	Earplug
	Shower water bag
	Shower Cap
	Bath Towels
	Sunglasses
	Deodorant

Miscellaneous Checklist

Check	Listing
	Camera
	Camcorder
	Memory Card
	Campsite reservation
	Contact person and phone number
	Pet supplies and food
	Notebook/pen/pencil
	Sketch pads
	Umbrella
	Guide book
	Map
	Compass
	GPS receiver
	Travel alarm clock
	Cell phone
	Two Way Radio
	Sewing kits
	Kleenex
	Duct Tape
	Rope
	Newspapers
	Playing cards
	Some playing game

Other Checklist

Check	Listing

Itinerary

Date	Details

Itinerary

Date	Details

Itinerary

Date	Details

Itinerary

Date	Details

Budget Plan

Pay for	Amount

Budget Plan

Pay for	Amount

Budget Plan

Pay for	Amount

Budget Plan

Pay for	Amount

My Journal

My Journal

My Journal

My Journal

My Journal

My Journal

My Journal

My Journal

My Journal

My Journal

My Journal

My Journal

My Journal

My Journal

My Journal

My Journal

My Journal

My Journal

My Journal

My Journal

My Journal

My Journal

My Journal

My Journal

My Journal

My Journal

My Journal

My Journal

My Journal

My Journal

My Journal

My Journal

My Journal

My Journal

My Journal

My Journal

My Journal

My Journal

My Journal

My Journal

My Journal

My Journal

My Journal

My Journal

My Journal

My Journal

My Journal

My Journal

My Journal

My Journal

My Journal

My Journal

My Journal

My Journal

My Journal

My Journal

My Journal

My Journal

My Journal

My Journal

My Journal

My Journal

My Journal

My Journal

My Journal

My Journal

My Journal

My Journal

My Journal

My Journal

My Journal

My Journal

My Journal

My Journal

My Journal

My Journal

My Journal

My Journal

My Journal

My Journal

My Journal

My Journal

My Journal

My Journal

My Journal

My Journal

My Journal

My Journal

My Journal

My Journal

My Journal

My Journal

My Journal

My Journal

My Journal

My Journal

My Journal

My Journal